The Poetry Of Robert Nichols
Volume 3 Poems & Phantasies

Robert Malise Bowyer Nichols was born in September 1893.

Robert was educated at Winchester College and then Trinity College, Oxford. In September 1914 with the shadow of the Great War covering Europe he enlisted, despite poor health, with the Field Artillery. He trained for a year and reached the front line just before the beginning of the Battle of Loos in September 1915. He was also to serve at the Battle of the Somme as an artillery officer in 1916, after suffering from shell shock he was invalided back to England.

Taking up service with The British Ministry of Labour and the Ministry of Information he began to write more avidly. As one of the War's surviving poets he was able to also give his work a depth and reflection that many of his other fallen contemporaries were not able too. He also began to give readings of his poems as well as tours in America.

Robert also wrote four plays and two novels as well as several further volumes of poetry. Now rightly regarded as one of the pre-eminent War Poets his poetry is richly rewarding, filled with vivid descriptions and emotions of the human suffering during war.

It's end brought him together with Nancy Cunard who was the inspiration for his next book Aurelia (1920). He was in Tokyo from 1921 to 1924 teaching English Literature and from 1924 to 1926 Hollywood beckoned.

In 1928 his play, Wings Over Europe, foretelling the splitting of the atom was a success in New York. In 1933-4 he was in Austria and Germany, his long weekly letters to Henry Head, the neurologist under whose care he had been for shell-shock, give a graphic eye-witness account of the rise of Hitler.

By the end of the 1930's he was living in the South of France, his emotional and financial affairs in turmoil. With occupation of France by German and Vichy forces he was on the last ship to carry British refugees from the Cote d'Azur.

Robert Nichols died on December 17th 1944. He is buried at St Mary's, in Lawford, Essex.

Index Of Poems

A TRIPTYCH

I. FIRST PANEL: THE HILL
On a day in Maytime mild
Mary sat on a hill-top with her child.
(Overhead in the calm sky's arching
The curled white clouds went slowly marching....
But underneath the blue abyss
All was stiller than water is
Leagues under the surface of the sea.)

And all about her thick and free
Blossomed the dear familiar flowers.
There, while her boy played through the hours,
And the high sun shook gold upon her,
Mary plaited a garland in his honour
Who should be the King of Kings;
And when 'tis done this song she sings,
As Jesus, tired and happy, rests
Curled in the hollow of her breasts:

"In the shadow of my dress,
Out of the sun
And his fierce caress,
Sleep, my son.

"Soft the air about the hill,
Scented, sunny, clear, and still;
Below in the woods the daffodil
Nods, and the shy anemone
Creeps up from the thicket to look on thee,
And ten thousand daisies meet
In an ocean of stars about thy feet.

"Daisies have I strung for thee,
Darling boy,
Wee white blossoms that shall be
Dappled, ah! so rosily
With thy blood,
When they nail thee to the wood
Cleft from out the crooked tree.
Can it be,
Daisies innocent and good,
That ye star black Calvary?

"Buttercups I make thy crown,
Darling boy.
(Lullaby, O lullaby!)
Son of sorrow, son of joy,
Pain and Paradise thou art,
Thou that sighest nestling down
In my breast, over my heart
That is a lake
Where the hidden tear-drops ache
To be free,
Till mounting upward for thy sake
Out they break,
Down they plash on me and thee.

"And Heaven in her charity
Drops seven tears on me and thee.

"This thy little childhood's crown,
Flower on flower,
Wear thou in thy lullaby
Till thou facest the soldiers' frown
In thine iron hour,
Till the thorn they crown thee by
They press down:
Ah, the sharp points in my heart!
Ah, the sword, the sudden smart
Flaying me as 'twere a flame!
Crowned indeed, my son, thou art
With red flowers of pain and shame!

"Birds and butterflies and trees,
And the long hush of the breeze
Shimmering over the silken grass,
What wouldst thou have more than these?...
In the stall the ox and ass
Gazed on thee with tender eyes;
All things love thee; yet there lies
Some hid thing in thee breeds fear
Brims not falls thy mother's tear.
Wherefore, baby, must thou go?
Rose, to be torn in sunder so?
Little bonny limbs, little bonny face,
My lamb, my torment, my disgrace!

"O baby, are thine eyelids closed
Faster than my eyes supposed?
With foxes must thy bed be maken,
A beggar with beggars must thou go,
To be at last forsworn, forsaken?
And bear alone thy cross also
Anigh to the foot of a bare hill?
To hang gibbeted and abhorred,
For passers-by to wish thee ill?
And to thrust against thy will
Through thy mother's bosom the sharpest sword?

"O baby, breathing so quietly,
Have thou mercy upon me!
That in thy madness
On thy lonely journey farest,
That understandest not nor carest
For me and my sadness!
Woe indeed! thou dost not know
Man cometh into this world in sorrow
To spend in grief to-night, to-morrow
In sorrow the third day to go!

"O sleep, dear baby, and, heart, sleep;

Turn to thy slumber, golden, deep,
Of present possible happiness.
Let drop the daisies one by one
Over his body and his dress;
Afflicted eyes, see but thy son
Who sleeps secure from hurt, from harm,
Clasped to my breast, closed in my arm,
Who murmurs as the flowers by the faint wind shaken,
And, putting forth sweet, sleepy hands,
Feels for the kisses he demands....
Slowly, belov'd, dost thou awaken,
And sure, in heaven there is no sign:
It is not true that thou shalt be taken,
Who forever, forever art mine, art mine!"

Into the west the calm white sun
Floated and sank. The day was done.
Mary returned, and as she went,
Above her, in the firmament,
The stars, that are the flowers of God,
Mirrored the flowery earth she trod.
Thus bore she on her destined child,
And while she wept, behold! he smiled,
And stretched his arms seeking a kiss....
Softly she kissed him, and a bliss,
Deeper than all her human tears,
Flooded her and put out her fears.

OXFORD,
Early Spring, 1914.

II. SECOND AND CENTRE PANEL: THE TOWER
It was deep night, and over Jerusalem's low roofs
The moon floated, drifting through high vaporous woofs.
The moonlight crept and glistened silent, solemn, sweet,
Over dome and column, up empty, endless street;
In the closed, scented gardens the rose loosed from the stem
Her white showery petals; none regarded them;
The starry thicket breathed odours to the sentinel palm;
Silence possessed the city like a soul possessed by calm.

Not a spark in the warren under the giant night,
Save where in a turret's lantern beamed a grave, still light:
There in the topmost chamber a gold-eyed lamp was lit
Marvellous lamp in darkness, informing, redeeming it!
For, set in that tiny chamber, Jesus, the blessed and doomed,
Spoke to the lone apostles as light to men entombed;
And spreading his hands in blessing, as one soon to be dead,
He put soft enchantment into spare wine and bread.

The hearts of the disciples were broken and full of tears,
Because their lord, the spearless, was hedgëd about with spears;
And in his face the sickness of departure had spread a gloom,
At leaving his young friends friendless.
They could not forget the tomb.
He smiled subduedly, telling, in tones soft as voice of the dove,
The endlessness of sorrow, the eternal solace of love;
And lifting the earthly tokens, wine and sorrowful bread,
He bade them sup and remember one who lived and was dead.
And they could not restrain their weeping.
But one rose up to depart,
Having weakness and hate of weakness raging within his heart,
And bowed to the robed assembly whose eyes gleamed wet in the light.
Judas arose and departed: night went out to the night.

Then Jesus lifted his voice like a fountain in an ocean of tears,
And comforted his disciples and calmed and allayed their fears.
But Judas wound down the turret, creeping from floor to floor,
And would fly; but one leaning, weeping, barred him beside the door.
And he knew her by her ruddy garment and two yet-watching men:
Mary of Seven Evils, Mary Magdalen.
And he was frighted at her. She sighed: "I dreamed him dead.
We sell the body for silver...."
Then Judas cried out and fled
Forth into the night!... The moon had begun to set;
A drear, deft wind went sifting, setting the dust afret;
Into the heart of the city Judas ran on and prayed
To stern Jehovah lest his deed make him afraid.

But in the tiny lantern, hanging as if on air,
The disciples sat unspeaking. Amaze and peace were there.
For his voice, more lovely than song of all earthly birds,
In accents humble and happy spoke slow, consoling words.

Thus Jesus discoursed, and was silent, sitting upright, and soon
Past the casement behind him slanted the sinking moon;
And, rising for Olivet, all stared, between love and dread,
Seeing the torrid moon a ruddy halo behind his head.

GRAYSHOTT,
July, 1914.

III. THIRD PANEL: THE TREE
The crookëd tree creaked as its loaded bough dipped
And suddenly jerked up. The rope had slipped,
And hideously Judas fell, and all the grass
Was soused and reddened where he was,
And the tree creaked its mirth....
Mid the hot sky
Appeared immediate dots tiny and high,

Till downward wound in batlike herds
Black, monstrous, gawky birds,
And, narrowing their rustling rings,
Alit, talons foremost. And with flat wings
Flapped in the branches, and glared, and croaked and croaked,
While no compassionate human came and cloaked
The thing that stared up at the giddy day
With pale blue eyeballs and wry-lipped display
Of yellow teeth closed on the blue, bit tongue.
Overhead the light in silence hung,
And fiercely showed the sweaty, knotted hands
Clutching the rope about the swollen glands....
And the birds croaked and croaked, evilly eyeing
The thing so lying,
Which no commiserate pity came and cloaked,
But which soaked
The earth, so that the flies
Dizzily swung over its winkless eyes,
And in a crawling, shiny, busy brood
Blackened the sticky blood,
And tickled the tongue-choked mouth that sought to cry
Bitterly and beseechingly
Against the judgment of th' unflinching sky.

The poor dead, lonely thing had not a shroud
From that still, frightful glare until a cloud
Of darkness, flowing like a dye
Over the edges of the sky,
Browned and put out the silent sun:
A benison
Of three hours' space.
And it had power
To put a shadow into that thing's face,
And th' invisible birds fell silent by its grace.

Thus Judas lay in shadow and all was still....
Then faint light, like water, began again to fill
The sky, and a whisper came it from the grass,
Whispering dry and sparse,
Or from the air beyond the neighbouring hill?
Ebbed, as a spirit on a sigh
Passing beyond alarm:
"It is finished!"
And there was calm
Under the empty tree and in the brightening sky.

GRAYSHOTT,
July, 1914.

FOUR SONGS FROM "THE PRINCE OF ORMUZ"

I. THE PRINCE OF ORMUZ SINGS TO BADOURA

When she kisses me with her lips, I become
A Roc, that giant, that fabulous bird
And over the desert, vast, yellow, and dumb,
I wheel, and my jubilant screaming is heard,
A voice, an echo, high up and glad,
Over the domes and green pools of Bagdad.

But when she kisses me with her eyes,
My heart melts in me; she is my sun;
She strokes my snow; I am loosed, I arise:
A brook of water I run, I run,
Crystal water, sunny and sweet,
Laughing and weeping to fawn at her feet.

LAWFORD,
Easter, 1914.

II. THE SONG OF THE PRINCESS BESIDE THE FOUNTAIN

My rose, or ever the three tears were shed
I wished lie in its bosom, has fallen apart;
Off their knapped golden hair all my pure pearls have sped
Before their mid-ruby could burn on my heart.
To-day is as yesterday; as to-day so to-morrow;
But fallen my rose, pearls, tears,
Fallen in sorrow.
Or ever I woke it was sunset to-day;
As fast flows the fountain, as fast flows away,
As fast fall away
My rose and my tears, my pearls and my sorrow.

IN HOSPITAL,
January, 1916.

III. THE SONG OF THE PRINCE IN DISGUISE

The look in thine eyes can change me utterly;
Thine eyes challenge: my heart is lighted,
I am thy taper, I burn straight-pointed
Ay, even so doing I waste away.

Bathe me in thy calm eyes' soft glances;
I am thy slave, I bow, I worship;
Bid me to steal, and I will steal gladly:
Ah! bid me not, thou robbest my manhood.

Let thine eyes smile: change comes upon me,
I put forth blossoms, flowers of my passion,
Roses crimson, alas! whose petals,

Once white, now blush with blood of my heart.

Gaze not on me: I burn, I perish;
Gaze not on me: I am thy servant;
Gaze not on me: I sink a-bleeding;
Yet gaze! I cannot otherwise live.

LAWFORD,
Easter, 1914.

IV. THE PRINCESS BADOURA'S LAST SONG TO HER LOVER
I have poured my wine into a gold cup,
I have plucked my roses, unfastened the stone
From my bosom. Thou mayest drink my red wine up,
Or spill where my jewel and roses are thrown.

The golden-globed night deepens quickly over
Me, afraid under its curtains. The spheres
Stare. O gather me swiftly, my lover;
Make me forget and forgive me these tears.

LAWFORD,
Easter, 1914.

THE GIFT OF SONG
Beyond a hill and a river,
Within a tower of stone,
A Princess by a casement
Dreamed, sitting still, alone.

Her golden hair hung heavy
Over her kirtle green;
Her eyes were blue and lonely,
Her tender mouth had been

A joy for splendid kisses,
It was so red, so red;
But it was parted in singing,
And, beginning her song, she said:

"Three songs in my spirit:
Elusive, tremulous, light.
If you can feel their tremor,
This gift is spended aright."

Without in the silent garden
The sunflowers dozed in the sun,
Bees blackened their tawny faces,

Their heads drooped one by one.

Amid a stilly fig-tree,
Hidden from sun and sight,
A nightingale sang over
The songs that rejoice the night.

And browsing upon sweet grasses
In the fair solitude,
Half in sun, half in shadow,
A lordly bay stag stood.

Upon earth all was silent
Save when the hid bird sung;
In the dark blue afternoon heavens
A silent half-moon hung.

As she commenced singing,
The nightingale stopped. In the dead
Silence the leaves flicked softly;
The great stag turned his head.

Thus sung she alone, and only
The stag, the fig-tree, the bird
And pensive moon in the darkling heavens
Her lovely singing heard.

And as she finished singing,
She bowed her golden head
Low, O low, on her shaking bosom,
And, ending her song, she said:

"Three songs in my spirit:
Elusive, tremulous, light.
You have felt their tremor;
This gift is spended aright."

The nightingale lifted her voice up,
The moon fled out of the skies,
The fig-tree split, and two tears rolled
Out of the great stag's eyes.

Now, when she had done singing,
She closed her eyes, and her breath
Went out as she lay down backward
And folded her hands in death.

LYME REGIS,
July 6, 1916.

FRAGMENTS FROM A DRAMA ON THE SUBJECT OF ORESTES

I. WARNING UNHEEDED

Kassandra.
I cried in the halls where the feast will be set;
The hurrying servants whom I met
Brushed me aside, asked why I tarried.
On their black woolly heads gold platters they carried,
Piled high with rich fruits; betwixt jewelled hands,
Goblets of crystal, white blossoming wands,
Urns breathing incense: all these to be set
Where Truth's feast and the feasters too soon shall be met.

The guest shall turn as he laughs and sups,
Reaching his hand for the golden wine;
His face shall change as he sees next to him
A mouth that mocks, eyes that look through him,
A head sink her glistening brow 'twixt the cups,
Locks blackening his stoup with a liquor of brine.

In the scrolls of the platter of gold there has bled
The juice of fruit battered and hairy and red;
The goblets of crystal are fissured and cracked
Like ice the bronze tyre of the chariot has wracked,
And the blossoms curl withered because of the heat
Of urns overset by the slip of red feet
When the reveller fell forward unable to save
His eyes from the torch, his groin from the glaive.

Chorus.
For Truth rejected returns as Pain.

Kassandra.
Under the trestles the guests lie slain;
The curtains upon the gold cords pull
Heavily, sagging like nets that are full,
For curved in the trough and propped in the fold
The red, red catch lies tossed and rolled;
The halls and corridors reek with the flood;
The pillars are trickled with cyphers of blood;
Rent garlands lie trampled over the floors;
Rusty footprints lead out through the high bronze doors
To the starlit night and the whispering plain:

Chorus.
For Truth rejected returns as Pain.

Kassandra.
I weep for the ruin of a high, proud house;

Moths fret the still curtains; down the throne runs a mouse;
The sun fades on the floors heaped high with dead leaves;
The moon runs on the rills that run from the eaves;
Brown clogs the peristyle; the air has a tang;
Weeds rot on the terrace; the hanging gates clang;
The wind is a weariness; man lives in vain

Chorus.
Where Truth rejected returns as Pain.

1914-1916.

II. ORESTES TO THE FURIES

Ye are no madman's dreams, then!...
Out sword! Backward tread
O curs that circle the bright blade ye dread.
Back to where dead-eyed Hate, your shameful priest,
Prepares your bowl of blood, your fleshy feast:
Where in the thronged and long-hushed marketplace
Ten thousand faces gaze on one pale face;
Where the lost victim feels the lonely ban
Of death terrific loosed by man on man;
Where black blood froths, where drives the whirring wheel;
Where hands, ears, lips fall lopped of instant steel;
Where the intent and dazzling pincher plies
Till to the silent tortures Anguish cries
At once for death! and when sharp death is given,
Others, corded and swooned, antic and sick, are driven
Under the axe, whose sheeny flash and fall
Bids the block ring as pile beneath the maul,
Till Man's protest dies to a whisper, dumb
Beneath the maddened rolling of Death's drum!

1915.

BLACK SONG

I. AT BRAYDON

Day wanes slowly;
On the hill no sound
Save the wind uttering
Chords low ... few ... profound.

How the west smokes and quivers!
It sears, it blinds my sight;
I am burned out wholly,
Hide me from the light.

Within dear arms yoke me,

Gather me. I am sped
Into your little bosom
Press, hide my childish head.

How long I have struggled
I know not; but the past
Seems twice livelong,
Beaten at the last!

My soul leaps and shudders
In pain none understands;
With your clear voice calm it,
Soothe it with your hands.

I can say only
So lost am I, so distressed
"I love you: I am tired."
You must guess the rest.

I love you: I am tired.
I give you my soul,
It hurts me. Hate has lamed it.
Take it; make it whole.

Late Summer, 1916.

II. MIDDAY ON THE EDGE OF THE DOWNS
Stillness falls and a glare.
The woods in darkness lie.
The fields are stretched and stare
Under the empty sky.
Vacant the ways of the air,
Along which no birds fly.
Only the high sun's flare
Spills on the empty sky.

I lift my aching eyes
From the dry wilderness:
Across me a peewit flies
With gestures meaningless....
Mine are his piping cries
At this world's emptiness!

1913.

III. IN DORSETSHIRE
Cold and bare the sunlight
Drifted across the hill,
Round which the sea wind's current

Unfathomable and chill,
From dawn to silver sunset
Poured now faint, now shrill.

"How to comfort you,
Share any part?
Even to understand you
Too deep an art!
Yet I'd comfort you,
Tear out my heart."

"Do not look on me,
Dry eyes for my sake;
Do not smooth my forehead
Your hands make me ache;
O, and turn away your kisses
Or heart must break."

Cold and bare the sunlight
Drifted across the hill,
Only the sea-wind's current,
Unfathomable and chill,
Heard such speech gather,
Bewail itself ... fall still.

Toward the hill then zigzagged
One wind-harried plover
Rocked for a moment....
Cried to love and lover
The top of loneliness
Ere he heeled over.

MAN'S ANACREONTIC AND OTHER POEMS

MAN'S ANACREONTIC
Kiss! Kiss me and kiss again,
Make kissing almost pain;
Close your fingers close on mine,
And our grappling looks entwine;
Kiss again, and when that's done
Blind me with each facing sun
Of your clear and golden eyes,
Till my spirit in me dies,
And endures a long eclipse
Till rekindled at your lips.

From this minute I pursue
The intense Idea that's you
Your you's Being. I would draw

You from Obscurity's dusk maw
Into my hands whate'er you are,
Moth or spirit, gnome or star.
Yet I would not filch a part,
Misty soul or flaming heart,
Which left but, as doth the snake,
A pale tissue. I will take
And shut all your sweetness up
In the gold walls of a cup,
Sandalled feet to sweeping hair,
Soul, brain, body, all you are
Curled as a mermaid coiled in brine,
Now drunk one gush of giddy wine!

Nay, as a strange lump of snow
In my two hands you shall go,
And I'll bare my browny breast,
Press you there, where now you rest!
Ay, and bless the frozen smart
As you melt into my heart!

Come, I'll twine you round my brows:
A defiant diadem,
Poets of your light shall sing.
Satraps by you swear stout vows
Eyeing my twice-marvellous gem
You: the emerald in my ring.

Thus I'll keep you night and day,
Since no stone can run away
And might dare a pleasure splendid:
Toss my ring into the air,
Watch it spinning, heart suspended,
Lest it slip me unaware,
Fall clean through my finger bars,
Shatter in ten thousand stars!
Yet you shall not be my ring;
You shall not be anything,
Crown or stone set cunningly,
Time can separate from me.

No! I'll find an alchemist,
With a beard of cobwebs grey
And fired eyes like moonstones kissed
By the last gold beam of day,
And older and gentler than a fish,
And wiser than an elephant;
And when I've told him what we wish,
Bribe or force him work our want.

We two shall opposëd stand,

Each touch other's finger-tip;
At a slow pass of his hand
And a soft word from his lip,
We will incline smilingly,
And as drops together run,
Shaking off the he and she,
Close and be forever one.

GRAYSHOTT,
Summer, 1914.

THE BLACKBIRD

I stand in a sunny garden;
A blackbird sings overhead:
"I'm alive ... I've a love ... the sun's shining
And where's the man would be dead?"

"Blackbird, make an ending of fluting
That song down your orange beak:
I'm alive ... I've a love ... the sun's shining,
And I am the man you seek."

STAMFORD,
May, 1913.

CHANGE

Behold, the tides are awake!
Under the high moon's light,
Broad bands of silver, they glitter and quake,
Moving out into the night.

Off from the shore they slide,
Out, out into the blue:
And I am turned to a shimmering tide
Flooding on outward to you!

HENGISTBURY HEAD,
Spring, 1915.

TRANSFIGURATION

Two feet apart, straight-limbed on the heathered hill
We lie, under the wavering haze
Of the sun, even as two logs that lie still
In the heart of a blaze.
Side by side we lie through the long
Late noon together;
On us the light wind stoops his strong,
Hot, sweet scents of heather.

No word breaks the air that smothers,
Lest we miss
The dull heart-beat of the earth below each other's,
And the soft kiss
Of breathless heather upon heather, while the sun
Beats on us encouraging the swiftening blood,
Till up the limbs and through the ears it run,
A thin, red singing flood.

Love hath put in me might,
That was so weak;
I am strong with light,
My senses seek
Something indefinable, afar;
They go wandering, and return....
With the light drunk off a star
They calmly burn,
Even as the immense sun burns on us
Till evening turns watery those beams of his;
And, rising from that joyance onerous,
I stoop a kiss
Lighter than the balls of fluff
The wind sways across the heath,
Though each invisible, hot puff
Scarce rocks a spray beneath.

I sit, and it is so still,
Now wind and sun have gone home,
I can almost hear distil
The dew in the gloam.
And from the clear and cool
Of the twilit air,
That is still as a pool
Iced over and bare,
I catch at length
The thought I have been searching for:
Did I absorb the sun's or just your strength,
Or Something More?

Summer, 1914.

PLAINT OF PIERROT ILL-USED
I am Pierrot, and was born
On some February morn
When through glistering rain shone down
The full moon on Paris town.
(Ah the moonshine in my head!)

For, upon the fatal minute
When the moon's heart changes in it

And the tides their flow reverse,
I, for better or for worse,
Born was. (Better been born dead
Than with moonwork in my head!)

Clown stood foster, but another
Got me of Clown's wife my mother,
And as suited my poor station,
Thieving was made my profession:
Doorsteps often were my bed
(Frosty moonshine in my head).

Yet while Pierrot was a thief
Miracle beyond belief,
Chance fantastic as divine!
I fell in with Columbine:
Dark eyes, lips of mournful red
(Dark-bright moonshine in my head).

At the corner of the street
She and I by night would meet;
Met, but never told our love,
While th' ironic moon above
In her reverie smiled, and shed
Tranquil radiance round each head.

Till my father by a breath
Stifled at the hands of Death,
"Since no other children were
Assigned me as only heir."
(Silver sequins heaped and spread:
Billowing silver in my head.)

So, in search of fitting knowledge,
Poor Pierrot was sent to college,
Where Pantaloon and Pantaloon
In answerless riddles o' the moon
Crammed more moonshine in his head.

Home, then, Pierrot by-and-by
Hurried spent, resolved to sigh
Headache, heartache, and the rest,
Out on Columbine's white breast,
White as the moon's cloudy bed
(Hush the moonshine in my head).

But, while gone, had entered in
Spangled, smiling Harlequin;
Laughter cynic and unholy:
"Pah! Pierrot's poor melancholy!"
Turned but not a word I said

(Moons like swords within my head!)

Forth: but money burns so bright!
Let it burn, then, left and right:
"Where, O where, is Punchinello?
Scaramouch too, that gay fellow?
A brisk life it is we'll lead:
Drown the moonshine in my head!"

Midnight: Venus by an urn,
Roses and rose lanterns burn,
Wine, fount's purl, and mandoline....
Pulcinella waits within,
Faithless she but in her bed:
No more moonlight in my head!

Ah!...
yet dawns a dreary morrow:
'Spend at ease, and owe in sorrow,'
With light purse to her begone,
If but as a hanger-on!
(Dread and moonlight in my head.)

Home then: catch upon the way
'Harlequin fled yesterday.
Bankruptcy of his employ.'
Surging of relief and joy:
Welcome then? past words unsaid?
Surge of moonlight through my head.

So on, beating, to her street:
What sight Pierrot's eyes doth greet?
One coach at her door arrives,
From the back another drives....
Strange! (mere moonlight in the head).

Pull the bell: is she within?
'I must see Miss Columbine.'
Maid with finger laid by nose,
Better not inquire too close
Such puts bullets through the head!

Now I wander back and forth;
Pierrot goes east, south, west, north;
Shakes his head and shrugs his shoulders,
Till the more acute beholders,
Watching him, have hazarded,
'Touch of something in the head?'

I am Pierrot, and was born
On some far forgotten morn

When the cold moon on the pane
Struck and, signless, 'gan to wane,
When the tides their flow reversed;
And I bear, uncured, accursed,
Aching until I am dead,
Moonlight, moonlight in my head!

DEVONSHIRE,
November, 1916.

GIRL'S SONG FROM "THE TAILOR"[2]
[2] "The Tailor," opera-buffa in three acts, being Op. 10 of Bernard van Dieren.

O silver bird, fly down, fly down,
Bring thy fair gifts to him and me:
A purse contains a minted crown,
A golden ring for me.
Ah! lovely bird, fly down, fly down.

But upon the highest bough
See amid the leaves he swings,
Pipes three notes of laughter low,
Flirts, and folds his flashy wings.
Ah! lovely bird, fly down, fly down.

What is't, bird, thy soul demands?
Come, I'll rock thee in my breast;
I will stroke thee with my hands;
Where none rested thou shalt rest....
Ah! lovely bird, fly down, fly down.

Jewels wouldst thou, then, O bird?
See, among the sunny grass
A tear has fallen unseen, unheard,
Brighter than ever diamond was.

Hark! Hark! His joy my voice doth drown:
See, see, he leaps, floats, dives him down!

1916.

LAST SONG IN AN OPERA
From the apple bough many petals fly tossed of the wind,
Yet goldenly heavy it hangs on blue autumn eves
(All things come unto him whose heart believes).
The dove, though the tempest-swept sun her bright eyes blind,
Beats onward fast.
Till with clapped, sailing wings down at the last
To the loved cote she come.

Ah, the long way of Love, but Love comes home!

The silver river wanders and circles time out of mind,
Yet turns at length where the sea tosses her smoking sheaves
(All things come unto him whose heart believes).
So golden-feathered Love beats his high course, though blind,
Until that hour
When, downward stooping through the flaming shower,
Into the heart he come.
Ah, the long way of Love, but Love comes home!

1916.

DANAË

MYSTERY IN EIGHT POEMS

DANAË: MYSTERY IN EIGHT POEMS
I
"What with clangour, clangour of iron din,
Do they beat till daylight ring?
What heat, that I see the night air spin,
And sparks dance over the scaffolding?

"The birds have flown because of their strife
Hammering difficult metal;
Their reek has taken my roses' life,
Dripping white petal on petal.

"What glows gold taller than earthly tree
In that maze of mast on mast
Of the scaffolding? What can it be
They build so secret and fast?"

II
"What art mooning at, fool?
Some wanton boy and his limbs?
Such dreams should be put to school:
I'll chasten these fleshly whims!"

He has shot the bolts on her room
In the brazen tower.
"Remain there, ninny: your doom
Till the sand sifts your last hour!"

With eyes grieving on space,
Has she sight among all these blind?
Because of her dreaming face....
How harshly the great keys grind!

They have gone. She clenches her hands,
She struggles and makes soft moan....
Then smiles, for she understands:
The soul is never alone.

III
"Last night as I was sitting,
My faint heart ceased to beat,
Listening in the silence
To the tread of nearing feet.

"Through the tower dumb in midnight
They passed from floor to floor,
Till at length they halted
Hard without my door.

"I knew 'twas Thou who stood'st there,
With but a door's divide!
With a wild and longing motion
I strode and flung it wide.

"Out into velvet darkness
My whirring eyeballs stare.
I whisper. Nothing answers.
And there is no one there."

IV
CANTICLE
"O Day so bright,
Bring thou my Love to me,
In blinding, deep delight
And ecstasy.

"O Night so wide,
So black, keep close till He,
The light within my side
Seen, comes to me.

"O wandering Wind,
Sing in His ears the sum
Of longing, mad His mind,
Compel He come.

"Earth I adore,
From whom to whom I go,
Bring Him to me before
I return so.

"Sun, nought doth let
In journey or depart;
Make Him, arisen, set

Within my heart.

"O high white Moon,
Alone and glittering,
As you pull ocean soon,
My Belovëd bring.

"O swelling Sea,
Cavernous in your sweep,
Make Him ingulph, drown me
Far in His deep.

"O Day, O Night,
O Moon, O Sun, O Sea,
O Wind, bring my Delight!
Bring Him to me!"

V
In the second watch of the night
The amazed guards saw with affright
Gold stars fall in a shower:
Coins of gold in a sweeping flight,
They silently broke on the tower.

And the tower's top turned a rose
Of enwreathed, ruddy light,
And, like men smit of their foes,
The guards fell at the sight....

And the Rose possessed the tower alone
All the blue, windless night.

VI
"Soft torrential wind
Falls through the vast, still deep
Like thick dreams pouring behind
The opened gates of sleep:
Ah, not so swift, Lord, not so bright,
Lest I be blown, a feather;
Not so white, not so white,
Lest I be withered altogether.

"Earth shifts under my feet,
Glory breaks over my head;
Speechlessly my wings I beat,
And fall mute in breathless dread:
Ah, not so swift, Lord, not so bright,
Lest I be blown, a feather;
Not so white, not so white,
Lest I be wilted altogether."

VII

"Mine is a heavenly Lover,
In Him I am wholly blest;
My heart it is His coffer
Wherein His gold doth rest.

"Dead in the metal tower
I lie till night doth come,
When in a golden shower
He bursts the midnight dome.

"And, caught beyond releasing,
I yield me to His claim,
And by my creature ceasing
All that He is I am."

VIII

The silver sun looks down
On the silent tower;
The guards awaken, nor own
To the unguarded hour.

They eye each other's face,
But to speak none durst;
As though the night were ungraced,
Silent they are dispersed.

The cruel King climbs, doth draw
Near, then by he creeps,
Marking in rage and awe
The smile in which she sleeps.

STAMFORD,
Autumn, 1912, and Autumn, 1913.

THE ECSTASY

I lay upon a headland hill:
The sun spilt out his gold;
The wind blew with a fluttering thrill;
The skies were blue and cold.

All day above the little cove
I heard the long wind flow;
The clouds foamed in the blue above,
The blue sea foamed below.

All day the bare sun fiercely burned;
All day in the profound
And quivering grass my body turned,

One with Earth's turning round.

Till, fledged amid her fluid rings,
My soul began to rouse,
And slowly beat her silver wings
Within her darkened house.

Then with vans lifted up for flight,
With stretched and fiery crest,
Upward she leaped toward the light
And drew from out my breast.

How long I lay while she was fled,
And on the cliff below
My body lay stiff, dark, and dead,
I knew not nor may know.

But long it seemed. Sped beyond sight
My soul enjoyed release;
Beyond the clouds, within the light,
She entered into peace.

To-day, amid a world of men,
How often must I cry:
"Happy I never was but then
Nor shall be till I die!"

NEAR GOLD CAP,
Late Summer, 1916.

THE WATER-LILY

The Lily floated white and red,
Pouring its scent up to the sun;
The rapt sun floating overhead
Watched no such other one.

None marked it as it spread abroad
And beautifully learned to cease:
But Beauty is its own reward,
Being a form of Peace.

1913.

DEEM YOU THE ROSES....

Deem you the roses taste no pleasure
Unfolding hour by hour
Toward, through starlit peace and sunny leisure,
Their sharpest moment, when they dower
This great green world, this rustling place,

Active in music, light, and grace,
With their hid hearts, their golden treasure,
Odours so deep they overpower?

See how, hazed in the sunny weather,
The silken roses swim,
Nodding heads frail as a high cloud's feather,
Expressing Joy in Beauty's Hymn.
And, hark! from many a hidden face
Echoes I hear through silver space:
The Morning Stars that sing together,
And the delighting Seraphim!

LAWFORD,
Early Summer, 1916.

THE PASSION

Those whose Love, unborn to sight,
Never did itself disclose
Save in water's cry; a rose;
Meteor furrowing the night;

Mote of any turning ray;
Pipe of bird mid sunset's flush;
Rain stilled, leaves flame-wet, and hush
Of a rainbow's fire and spray;

Any straight road leads afar
'Cross a hill-brow. What's beyond?
Seven hung notes of music fond;
Seven dark poplars, one white star;

Cloud lifting a tower aloft;
Light and play and shadowy grace
Of the soul behind a face
Flitting by on motion soft;

Lonely figure on a height;
Those whose love but shines a hint
Fainter than the far sea's glint
To the inland gazer's sight

These alone, and but in part,
Guess of what my songs are spun,
And Who holds communion
Subtly with my troubled heart.

But the substance of my grief
Scarcely can their thought surmise,
Who but glimpse through these my eyes

Joy as fathomless as brief.

Others in this strange world flung,
Orphans, too, of Destiny,
Have the virtue, but not I,
Keeps heart crystal, single tongue;

And know not, whose hearts are whole,
How when sickened and unclean,
Unfit or to see, be seen
Close thorns pack and prick the soul.

Yet though here soul suffereth,
Complicate by vision's light,
Never would I cede this right
Of a sharpened life and death.

For I keep in confidence
In my breast a subtle faith
'Scapes alway by narrow scathe
And I draw my succour thence.

One Day, or maybe one Night
Living? dying? I shall see
The Rose open gloriously
On its heart of living light.

Know what any bird may mean,
Meteor in my heart shall rest,
Spelled on my brain blaze th' unguessed
Words of the rainbow's dazzling sheen.

O the hour for which I wait!
Lovers of the Secret Love
Watch with me, and we will prove
Constancy can be elate.

For the sigil we have now
Is but echo, shadow, less
Than a nothing's nothingness,
To what that hour will allow:

Lost and found! The Shining Ones!
Music, passion, scent, delight,
Light and depth and space and height:
Heaven and its seven suns!

DORSET SQUARE,
October, 1916.

LAST WORDS

O let it be
Just such an eve as this when I must die!
To see the green bough soaking, still against a sky
Washed clean after the rain.
To watch the rapturous rainbow flame and fly
Into the gloom where drops fall goldenly,
And in my heart to feel the end of pain.
The end of pain: the late, the long expected!
To see the skies clear in a sudden minute,
The grey disparting on the blue within it,
And on the low far sea the clouds collected.

In that deep quiet die to all has been,
To be renewed, to bud, to flower again:
My second spring! whose hope was nigh rejected
Before I go hence and am no more seen.

To hear the blackbird ring out, gay and bold,
The low renewal of the ringdove's moan
From among high, sheltered boughs, and ceaseless fall
Pitter, pitter, patter,
A dribble of gold
From leaves nodding each on the other one,
The hush, calm piping and the slow, sweet mood!
To drink the ripe warm scent of soaking matter,
Wet grass, wet leaves, wet wood,
Wet mould,
The saddest and the grandest scent of all.

So when my dying eyes have loved the trees
Till with huge tears turned blind,
When the vague ears for the last time have hearkened
To the cool stir of the long evening breeze,
The blackbird's tireless call,
Having drunk deep of earth-scent strong and kind,
Come then, O Death, and let my day be darkened.

I shall have had my all.

LAWFORD,
April, 1916.

Robert Nichols – A Concise Bibliography

Invocation (1915)
Ardours and Endurances (1917)
A Faun's Holiday & Poems & Phantasies (1917)
Sonnets to Aurelia (1920)
The Smile of the Sphinx (1920)

Fantastica: Being the smile of the Sphinx and other tales of imagination (1923)
Twenty Below (1926) with Jim Tully
Wings Over Europe (1928) play
Fisbo or the Looking Glass Loaned (1934) verse satire aimed at Osbert Lancaster
A Spanish Triptych (1936) poems
Such was My Singing (1942) poems